LIVING OUT LOUD
—— ON ——
PURPOSE!

*Finding Your Voice, Embracing
Your Identity, and Walking in Purpose*

KAREN F. HATCHER

Foreword by Dr. Barbara McCoo Lewis

River of Life
PUBLISHING

Unless otherwise noted, all Scripture quotations are taken from the King James Version (KJV) of the Bible.

Scripture quotations marked AMP are taken from the *Amplified® Bible*, copyright © 2015 by The Lockman Foundation. Used by permission. All rights reserved.

Scripture quotations marked NIV are taken from the *Holy Bible, New International Version®, NIV®*. Copyright © 1973, 1978, 1984, 2011 by Biblica, Inc.™ Used by permission. All rights reserved worldwide.

This book is a work of nonfiction. Any personal stories, examples, or testimonies included are used with permission or have been modified to respect privacy and preserve confidentiality.

Printed in the United States of America
ISBN: 978-1-968644-02-4
eBOOK ISBN: 978-1-968644-03-1

Hardcover ISBN: 978-1-968644-04-8

Library of Congress Control Number: 2025917887

River of Life Publishing
Memphis, Tennessee

Dedication

To my loving family, who have been my constant support and inspiration. To every person who has ever felt invisible, overlooked, or uncertain, this book is for you. May you find your voice, own your identity, and live boldly on purpose.

CONTENTS

Acknowledgments

First, I give all honor and glory to God—the One who called me out of silence and into purpose. Lord, thank You for Your unfailing love, relentless grace, and steadfast faithfulness toward me. Even when I questioned my worth, You affirmed my value. Even when I resisted the call, You pursued me with mercy.

Thank You for seeing something in me when I couldn't see it in myself—for calling me, forming me, and trusting me with this assignment. You shaped every word, guided every thought, and stood with me in every moment of this journey. This book is not just the work of my hands—it is the fruit of Your Spirit at work in my life.

May everything written here bring glory to Your name and draw hearts closer to You.

To my husband, Bishop Gabriel J. Hatcher Sr.—the love of my life, my greatest encourager, and my biggest fan. Thank you for more than just your unwavering love and support—thank you for seeing in me what I often couldn't see in myself. You've believed in my calling, challenged me to grow, and pushed me in ways you can't even imagine. Your strength has been a covering, your wisdom a guiding light, and your presence a steady place to land.

In moments when I wanted to shrink back, you reminded me to stand tall. In times of doubt, you spoke faith. Thank you for loving me through every season and for being the kind of husband who doesn't just walk beside me but lifts me higher.

To my children—Gabriel J. Hatcher II, Sarah Hatcher-James, and Rachel Hatcher-Collins—you are my world, my joy, and the place where I can be unapologetically and authentically me. Being your mother is one of the greatest honors of my life. Thank you for allowing me to grow, lead, love, and dream—while still being your mom. Your love, patience, and understanding have been a constant source of strength. You've cheered me on, held me up, and walked beside me in ways you may never fully realize.

To my wonderful parents, Elder Joe L. Gibbons and Supervisor Mable B. Gibbons—you were given the charge: "Train up a child in the way he should go: and when he is old, he will not depart from it." You did exactly what God instructed you to do concerning me, and that truth is undeniable. I pray that you can smile at the fruit of your labor and see the manifestation of your prayers. I know, without question, that the wife, mother, First Lady, and woman I am today is a direct reflection of how I was raised.

To my entire family, my siblings, Robin, Neci, Keith, and Sharon—thank you for your unwavering support, encouragement, and quiet confidence in who God has called me to be. Your belief in me, especially on the days I needed it most, has helped carry me through. I am who I am because of the foundation we share and the love that holds us together.

To my church family, Miracle Temple of Deliverance, you have been a source of love, growth, and accountability for me. You accept me with all of my idiosyncrasies and continue to undergird me in prayer. You have carried me from faith to faith and strength to strength. I pray that I will always serve you with humility, lead you with integrity, and love you with the heart of Christ. May my life and ministry reflect the same grace and encouragement you have so freely given to me.

To Bishop C.D. Williams and Bishop Phillip H. Porter, my fathers in the gospel, you poured so much into my spiritual upbringing and instilled within me the standard for holy living. Although I may not get it right every day, I know that you are in the great cloud of witnesses cheering me onward.

To my prayer companion, Margie Wilkins—those early morning walks have certainly paid off. Who would have known that our journey of prayer and holy conversations would lead me to this moment? You have been, and continue to be, a staple in my life, consistently reaffirming me with those simple yet powerful words: "Kay, God loves you!" You have taught me the value of dwelling in God's presence, the beauty of journaling, the richness of hymns, the strength found in quiet moments, and the power of offering unconditional positive regard. Thank you for your steady guidance that anchors my soul in faith.

To Jinnae Monroe, God placed you in my life at a time when I truly needed a push toward my next. Thank you for being the catapult—refusing to let my shyness keep you from pulling me closer to purpose. Your encouragement and boldness stirred something in me, and for that, I am eternally grateful.

To Jackie Harris, you walked with me through one of the most difficult and vulnerable seasons of my life. Your unwavering support, wisdom, and friendship were a lifeline. You are the epitome of true friendship—consistently reminding me to lift my eyes and never lose sight of the bigger picture.

To Prophetess Sharon Seay, a powerful force to be reckoned with—thank you for speaking over, through, and in my life, things that I couldn't see or even acknowledge. I will always cherish the indelible impact you continue to have on my journey.

To my Denver Family, Doris, LaDora, and Sia, you embraced the little girl far away from home and became my forever family.

Last but certainly not least, I owe a debt of gratitude to my nephew, Darius J. Willis—you are an entire workhorse, but here we are at the finish line, and this labor of love is the completed product. From the moment I spoke to you about this book, you followed up with, "Let's go!" In retrospect, you have always been the promoter, encourager, and even the pusher-over-the-ledge kind of guy. You know how to get things done and ensure they are executed with excellence. Thank you.

Finally, to every friend and encourager who reminded me that my voice mattered—thank you for pushing me to write.

To my spiritual mentors and leaders who spoke life into me when I was afraid to speak for myself, thank you for seeing what God placed in me.

And to every reader holding this book—thank you for allowing me to speak into your life. May you discover the power of living out loud on purpose.

Foreword

Living Out Loud on Purpose: Finding Your Voice, Embracing Your Identity, and Walking in Purpose is a must-read. The Enemy seeks to silence God's daughters and sons through fear, comparison, and self-doubt. He uses intimidation to shrink your confidence and dim your light, but God's plan is for you to shine brightly, live boldly, and declare His truth unapologetically.

The author, Evangelist Karen Hatcher, is a woman of conviction, compassion, and clarity. She gives us a clarion call for the silent to speak, the hesitant to step forward, and the unsure to believe again. The message is simple yet powerful: you have a voice, an identity, and a God-given purpose.

This writing is timely and prophetic. It speaks directly to this moment in history when God is raising up voices from the margins, callings from the shadows, and purpose from the ashes. Through Scripture, stories, and Spirit-led encouragement, it breaks chains, ignites courage, and restores confidence.

To every reader, you will be challenged not to shrink back. Do not let fear masquerade as humility. Don't allow intimidation to muzzle the voice God has given you.

As you read this book, your spirit will be stirred, your thinking will be challenged, and your walk will be strengthened.

Dr. Barbara McCoo Lewis
General Supervisor
International Department of Women
Church Of God In Christ, Inc.

Preface

The journey to *Living Out Loud on Purpose* began over 25 years ago. I had just stepped away from the comfort and familiarity of home to embark on a new chapter—as a young wife, a mother of three, and, now, a pastor's wife. My husband's first assignment was in Great Falls, Montana. During a revival there, the guest preacher spoke words that would mark me forever: "You're going to write a book."

I was stunned. I couldn't let on just how surprised—or captivated—I was by that prophecy. "Who, me?" I thought. *Little ole me?* I was a shy, unassuming introvert still in the process of discovering who I was, quietly managing the responsibilities of a new season in life.

Just a few days later, the title *Living Out Loud on Purpose* was birthed into my spirit. I knew it was more than a passing thought; it was a seed. Yet, for years, that seed lay dormant. The title itself had a peculiar, almost mysterious ring to it—compelling, yet unclear. I couldn't have imagined then how deeply connected it was to the journey of self-discovery and divine purpose that awaited me.

It would take years—through seasons of growth, hiddenness, heartache, and awakening—for the meaning behind that title to unfold. And it would take even longer for me to understand that God was not just giving me a book title—He was calling me into an identity, into an assignment, into a way of life.

There was a time when I felt invisible. Not in a dramatic or attention-seeking way, but in the quiet, overlooked corners of life—those moments when you wonder if your presence truly matters. For years, I faithfully fulfilled the roles of daughter, sister, wife, and mother, all beautiful and sacred. Yet, while giving and doing, it became easy to lose sight of the unique calling God had placed on *my* life.

Then came the divine disruption. A holy prompting shook me from my silence. I realized I was not created to blend in—I was created to stand out. I was not made to shrink back; I was made to *live out loud* and do it *on purpose*.

This book is the testimony of that awakening. It's a journey from invisibility to intentionality, from silence to significance, from passivity to purpose. But more than that—it's an invitation. An invitation for *you* to find your voice. To own your identity. To walk boldly in your God-given assignment.

Whether you're stepping out for the very first time or reawakening dreams that have been buried beneath doubt and delay, I pray these pages stir something in you. I pray they ignite a fire that will not be silenced. Because you, too, were made to live out loud. On purpose.

Introduction

God calls us to live with intentionality—to live purposefully for Him. From the way we conduct our lives to the way we love, from how we pray to how we praise—purpose is woven into every part of the believer's journey. That's why God gave us His Word. That's why He invites us to prayer. That's why He welcomes our praise. When we live intentionally, we do so in alignment with heaven.

This book is more than pages and principles—it's a call. A call to rise, to awaken, and to walk boldly in the identity God has already placed within us. Psalm 139 reminds us that we are fearfully and wonderfully made, intricately known, and divinely designed. God's Word tells us everything we need to know about ourselves—our worth, calling, purpose, and destiny.

Jeremiah 29:11 affirms that God already has a plan for us—an expected end. In that promise, we find assurance that our steps are not only ordered by God, but they are also authored by Him. God already has a plan, a blueprint leading us to His ultimate purpose; one that is intentional and filled with hope. Your journey is not random. Your voice is not accidental. Your purpose is not optional. As I reflect on the heart behind this work, I am reminded of the divine reason you were born. There is a voice within you—God-given, heaven-ordained—that must not remain silent.

We are living in a time where distractions are loud, and the spirit of intimidation is real. The Enemy works overtime to silence God's daughters and sons through fear, comparison, and self-doubt. But I declare that you will not be silenced. The Word of the Lord still stands: "For God hath not given us the spirit of fear; but of power, and of love, and of a sound mind" (2 Timothy 1:7).

In a world filled with confusion and comparison, this book serves as a lifeline. It breaks the grip of fear, dismantles lies, and calls forth destiny. It reminds us that purpose is not a one-time event, but a daily journey of faith and obedience. Through the pages that follow, you'll be challenged to shake off fear, release timidity, and embrace the bold life God intended for you.

You'll be reminded that living out loud isn't about making noise, it's about living with clarity. It's about knowing who you are, whose you are, and why you're here. I believe this book will stir something in you—a holy fire to stop shrinking and start shining. To move beyond survival and step into supernatural significance. You weren't created to blend in. You were created to live, speak, lead, and move—on purpose.

Scripture offers us powerful examples of men and women who had to overcome fear, inadequacy, or rejection before walking fully in their purpose:

- Moses said, "I am not eloquent... I am slow of speech" (Exodus 4:10), but God promised him, "Now therefore go, and I will be with thy mouth, and teach thee what thou shalt say" (Exodus 4:12), and he became a deliverer.
- Gideon, hiding in fear, called himself the least in his family (Judges 6:15), yet the angel

of the Lord greeted him as a "mighty man of valor" (Judges 6:12).

- Deborah, a prophetess and judge, led Israel to victory when women were rarely seen in leadership (Judges 4:4-9; 5:1-31). She needed no permission to walk in what God had already ordained.

- Hannah, in deep anguish, cried out to the Lord (1 Samuel 1:10-18), and turned her pain into purpose by birthing Samuel, the prophet who would anoint kings (1 Samuel 1:19-20).

- The wise woman of Abel lifted her voice with discernment and courage to negotiate peace, saving her entire city (2 Samuel 20:16-22).

- Jeremiah believed he was too young to speak: "Ah, Lord God! behold, I cannot speak: for I am a child" (Jeremiah 1:6). But God responded, "Say not, I am a child… I have put My words in thy mouth" (Jeremiah 1:7-9). and called him to be a prophet to the nations.

- Esther was positioned by God for influence, and her courage saved her people. Her uncle Mordecai declared, "And who knoweth whether thou art come to the kingdom for such a time as this?" (Esther 4:14).

- Mary, the young girl from Nazareth, surrendered to God's plan and said, "Be it unto me according to thy word" (Luke 1:38). Through her obedience, she carried the promise of salvation to the world.

- The Samaritan woman, once marked by shame, encountered Jesus at the well and found her voice. She boldly shared her testimony, and many believed because of her witness (John 4:7-30; 39-42).

- Peter, though he denied Jesus three times (Luke 22:54-62), was not disqualified. Jesus restored him, saying, "Feed My sheep" (John 21:15-17), and Peter preached the Gospel with power at Pentecost (Acts 2:14-41).

Each of these individuals experienced fear, uncertainty, or failure—yet God called them anyway. Their stories affirm that inadequacy, brokenness, or doubt do not disqualify us from divine purpose. In fact, they become sacred spaces where God's strength is made perfect. "My grace is sufficient for thee: for My strength is made perfect in weakness" (2 Corinthians 12:9).

There will be moments when the weight of your assignment feels heavy—when your past tries to disqualify you and the voices of fear attempt to silence you. But hear this truth: "I can do all things through Christ which strengtheneth me" (Philippians 4:13). That includes not only the comfortable and familiar, but also the stretching, unfamiliar, and faith-demanding things. You can overcome every obstacle the Enemy has used to try to hold you back. Through Christ, you will rise. You will endure. And you will thrive.

The same God who raised Esther for "such a time as this" is calling you now. Rise in courage. Stand in truth. Speak with love. Live out loud—on purpose.

This book will give language to your calling, ignite your faith, and empower you to stand in your God-given authority. Whether you are just discovering your voice or reclaiming it after a season of silence, these pages are for you. Let them inspire you, correct you, and most of all, propel you into the purpose that God has so beautifully crafted just for you.

I pray that you will not only find your voice, but that you will use it to glorify God and impact the world around you. May you no longer whisper where God has told you to roar. May you stop hiding what God has called you to carry. May you no longer dim your light to make others comfortable. Instead, rise in boldness, live in truth, and walk fully in the identity God has given you. So, take a deep breath. Lean in. Read every page with an open heart. Highlight, weep, pray, reflect—and most of all, apply. Let the Holy Spirit minister to you through these words. Let truth wash over every lie, and let purpose break through every delay. Get ready to live out loud—for real, for God, and forever. Let's go.

CHAPTER 1

You Did That on Purpose!

God does everything on purpose. This is one of the most powerful revelations we can ever receive when reflecting on His nature and power. Whether our life experiences are good, bad, or indifferent, God's hands are upon us. He is on target with His plans for our lives, and we can rest assured that He executes them with care and precision. Not only does He act with meticulous attention, but He also orchestrates our lives in a way that ultimately brings glory and honor to His name.

I'm reminded of an incident from my childhood when, while lining up after recess, mishaps often occurred. On one occasion, a classmate, hurrying to respond to the school bell, tripped and fell. She looked around, locked eyes with me, and snapped, "You did that on purpose!" Reflecting on it now, I realize she was accusing me of a deliberate act—one she believed was done with malicious intent. At the time, I was baffled by her words. She was suggesting that I had intentionally caused her fall, that my actions weren't accidental but deliberate, and worse, driven by malice. Nothing could have been further from the truth. She stumbled because she wasn't paying attention, not because of anything I did. But her words stuck with me, highlighting an important distinction: when something is done "on purpose," it implies intent, design, and often forethought.

As I reflect on that memory today, I see that the same phrase, "You did that on purpose," takes on a completely different meaning when applied to God. Unlike human actions, which can be motivated by flawed intentions, misunderstandings, or even accidents, God's actions are always deliberate and perfectly aligned with His divine plan.

Psalm 139 beautifully illustrates God's intentionality

toward us, His beloved creation. It highlights God's omniscience, omnipresence, and intimate involvement in every aspect of our lives, directly supporting the idea that He operates with intention and care.

Let's explore how Psalm 139 underscores God's intentionality:

1. God Knows Everything About Us

"You have searched me, Lord, and you know me. You know when I sit and when I rise; you perceive my thoughts from afar" (Psalm 139:1-2).

This passage reflects God's deep and personal knowledge of us. He is not distant or disconnected, but intimately aware of our every action, thought, and motive. Such intimate knowledge shows His intentionality in creating and guiding us according to His perfect plan.

2. God's Presence Is Everywhere

"Where can I go from your Spirit? Where can I flee from your presence?" (Psalm 139:7).

No matter where we are or what we face, God's presence surrounds us. His intentionality is evident in how He never leaves us to navigate life alone. Every step of our journey is within His sight and under His sovereign care.

3. God Designed Us with Precision

"For you created my inmost being; you knit me together in my mother's womb. I praise you because I am fearfully and wonderfully made; your works are wonderful, I know that full well" (Psalm 139:13-14).

The imagery of God "knitting" us together is a powerful testament to His intentionality. Like a skilled artisan, He crafted each of us with care, uniquely gifted, with purposes and roles to fulfill in His divine plan. We are not random or accidental; we are lovingly designed.

4. God's Plan Is Detailed and Purposeful

"Your eyes saw my unformed body; all the days ordained for me were written in your book before one of them came to be" (Psalm 139:16).

This verse emphasizes that every moment of our

lives is part of God's intentional plan. He has already written our stories, orchestrating each event to serve His greater purpose. Nothing in our lives happens outside of His knowledge or control.

5. God's Thoughts Toward Us Are Precious

"How precious to me are your thoughts, God! How vast is the sum of them!" (Psalm 139:17).

The psalmist marvels at the infinite care and attention God gives to each of us. His thoughts are deliberate, filled with love and concern for our well-being. This reinforces the truth that God's actions are never arbitrary but always purposeful.

When God does something "on purpose," it is neither haphazard nor careless. What He does, and what He allows, is deliberate, meaningful, and rooted in His infinite wisdom and love. The events of our lives—whether joyful, painful, or challenging—are not random. They are part of a greater narrative authored by God Himself. He uses every moment, every triumph, every setback, to shape us, teach us, and fulfill His ultimate purpose for our lives.

In my view, this is why the phrase "on purpose" is so powerful when applied to God. It reminds us that nothing in His plan is accidental or arbitrary. From the creation of the universe to the smallest details of our daily lives, everything God does is intentional. Genesis 1:31 captures this truth so wonderfully, encouraging us to this end, letting us know that when God finished creating the world, He didn't say, "Oops." There were no mistakes, no need for revisions, and no "do-overs." He didn't step back, scratch His head, and say, "I might need to fix that." Instead, He looked at His creation and declared it "good."

That same meticulous care and precision are evident in how He guides our lives. God doesn't make mistakes—and He never second-guesses His decisions. Nothing is accidental. His actions are always purposeful, aimed at fulfilling His divine will. Even when we don't understand His plan or feel overwhelmed by our trials, we can trust that God is working with the end in mind: our growth, His glory, and the ultimate good.

Living Out Loud is a call to live boldly for God, trusting that His intentions for our lives are good. Though we may not see the full picture now, He will make it clear in His perfect timing. It's a call to walk in faith—step by step—confident that He is leading us toward His purpose and glory.

It's a Strategic Operation

Have you ever seen a baby making its first attempts to walk? It's a strategic operation. The first efforts begin with finding balance. You see it, don't you? Those chunky legs and adorable feet, working to gain leverage. And then it happens—the arms flail, trying to steady the body until plop... down goes the baby onto its bottom and back to a crawling stance once again.

From that point on, it takes practice—repetition of leverage, balance, and flailing arms—before the art of putting one foot in front of the other becomes the norm. And when it finally happens, it's an illuminating experience.

Living out loud is ultimately a strategic operation

too, starting from the crawl of identity confusion, rising to the stumble of new understanding, and eventually walking with the steady stride of purpose. Every believer must embrace the process of growing into purpose. It isn't automatic. It requires moments of falling, getting back up, trying again, and trusting the guidance of the One who created you on purpose.

Living out loud on purpose means choosing to live as someone who has discovered that God has a purpose for you, and you are His purpose. It's embracing the truth that God's divine fingerprint is on your life. Moreover, He is calling you to live in a way that reflects His glory, grace, and greatness.

So, the next time life tries to trip you up and you find yourself questioning your steps, remember God did this on purpose. He allowed it, authored it, and is using it to build, shape, and launch you into the next level of your divine assignment.

Did you do that on purpose?

No, God did.

Purpose: The Age-Old Question

The question of purpose is as old as humanity itself. Psychologists, theorists, and scholars have long gathered at conferences and conventions, each seeking to unravel the complex mystery of why we exist. From ancient philosophers to modern thought leaders, purpose has remained a central, burning question—a longing etched into the soul of every human being. But for the believer, purpose isn't merely a concept to be debated; it is a divine assignment to be discovered and fulfilled.

To live out loud on purpose means living with intentionality—to exist with the full awareness that you are here for a reason. It's more than just surviving the day-to-day; it's about living with bold clarity, allowing your life to echo God's design for you on the earth. It's when your life becomes a statement—a declaration that you were created with value, vision, and victory in mind.

Living out loud is evidence that purpose has been discovered. It's the sound of dry bones responding to breath. It's the motion that follows revelation. It's what happens when someone who was once lifeless, directionless, and voiceless gets infused with identity and intention. When you finally know *why* you live, it begins to reshape *how* you live—marked by power, clarity, and courage.

Power: Empowered by Design

God's intention has always been that we live empowered. He never meant for us to navigate life in our own strength. That's why He gave us His Spirit—to dwell within us, to guide us into all truth, and to equip us with supernatural power.

Scripture says in Acts 1:8, "But you shall receive power when the Holy Spirit comes upon you." The same Spirit that raised Christ from the dead—the

same breath that filled the valley of dry bones in Eze-
kiel 37—is the power that now resides in us. Living
out loud begins with this power.

It's not about charisma or personality—it's about being connected to the One who called you. Purpose
without power is like having a car with no engine.
The Spirit of God is the engine that drives your destiny. He gives you the authority to walk boldly in
your calling and silences the lies that tell you you're
not enough.

Clarity: The Lens of Revelation
God gives us clarity. You can't live boldly in purpose
if you're unsure of your identity. Clarity allows you
to see yourself and your assignment through the lens
of revelation.

Psalm 119:105 says, "Your word is a lamp to my feet
and a light to my path." Clarity lights the way forward and helps you walk in alignment with your destiny.

When you gain clarity, you stop chasing comparison.
You stop mimicking someone else's mission. You

begin to realize that your lane has already been carved out by God—and your calling is to walk in it faithfully. Clarity brings peace to your process and confidence to your purpose.

Courage: Boldness in the Face of Resistance

And finally, you must have courage. To live out loud is to risk being seen. It means daring to be different in a world that thrives on imitation. It takes courage to rise when life has tried to keep you down. It takes courage to speak the truth in the face of opposition. Courage is the spiritual backbone that keeps you standing when everything around you says to sit and be quiet.

Living on purpose doesn't exempt you from challenges; it requires you to overcome them. There will be resistance. There will be moments of doubt. But when you are empowered by God and walking in clarity, courage through prayer becomes your posture. Not arrogance. Not performance. But holy boldness rooted in the unshakable assurance that God is with you.

Living out loud on purpose is not a suggestion; it's a calling. It is the outward expression of an inward revelation. It's the bold decision to rise from the ashes, speak from your spirit, and walk fully in the purpose for which you were created. When you live with power, clarity, and courage, you don't just exist— you live. And you live in such a way that others are inspired to do the same.

Reflection Questions

- In what areas of your life have you been living quietly or passively, instead of boldly and on purpose?
- How have you experienced the empowerment of God's Spirit in your everyday life?
- What steps can you take to gain greater clarity about your God-given purpose?
- What fears or challenges have been holding you back from living courageously?
- What does "living out loud" look like for you in this current season of life?

Let's Pray!

Dear Heavenly Father, breathe into me, Holy Spirit— revive every dry place and restore every broken piece of my life. Fill me with Your power, illuminate my path with clarity, and give me the courage to walk boldly in the purpose You've designed for me. I declare that I will no longer live in the shadows, but I will live out loud—on purpose and for Your glory. In Jesus' name. Amen.

CHAPTER 3

Becoming: Embracing the Process of Purpose

Before purpose becomes visible, it must be processed. The journey to becoming who God created you to be is not instant—it is layered, refined, and often painful. Becoming is the bridge between discovery and deployment. It's the messy middle. It's where God does His deep work in us so He can do a great work through us.

Too often, we want the platform without the process, the assignment without the alignment, the results without the refining. But God, in His wisdom, doesn't rush our becoming. He shapes, sifts, and sanctifies us in the unseen places so that when we emerge, we're not just prepared; we're proven.

Ecclesiastes 3:1 reminds us, "To everything there is a season, and a time to every purpose under the heaven." This verse isn't just poetic—it's prophetic. There is a *season* for becoming. And in that season, we learn to wait, yield, and grow. Waiting isn't wasted when you understand that God is cultivating something in you that can't be microwaved, because your purpose demands maturity and your destiny demands discipline.

The becoming season is where pride is crushed, patience is developed, and character is forged. Here is the proof. It's in the wilderness that Moses learned to lead. It's in the fields that David learned to worship and fight. It's in the pit and prison that Joseph learned to steward authority. Before God elevates you, He establishes you.

Becoming teaches you to surrender—not just your will, but your timeline. It's where you discover that the process *is* part of the purpose. God isn't just preparing the promise for you. He's preparing *you* for the promise.

So don't despise your process. Don't rush your becoming. What God is building in you during this season will sustain you in the next. Your yes in the quiet
qualifies you for the call in the spotlight.

Trust the process. Embrace the becoming. Because
on the other side of it, you'll be able to live out loud,
not just with passion, but with power, purpose, and
spiritual authority.

The Process Isn't Punishment

According to Genesis 50:20, "You intended to harm
me, but God intended it for good to accomplish what
is now being done, the saving of many lives." God
doesn't process us to punish us—He processes us to
prepare us.

Joseph's life is a masterclass in divine preparation.
He endured betrayal by his own brothers, endured
slavery, and sat in a prison cell for a crime he didn't
commit—all before stepping into his God-ordained
assignment in Egypt (Genesis 37–50). What looked
like a series of devastating setbacks was actually a
divine setup. Each trial was not random; it was re-

finement. God used every painful step to develop Joseph's character, sharpen his discernment, and prepare him for influence on a national scale.

There is a divine purpose behind every delay, every detour, and every discomfort. Preparation often feels like pruning—cutting away what is unnecessary so what remains can bear fruit. Just as Joseph had to be processed before his promotion, we too must walk through seasons of formation. God doesn't just prepare us for the platform. He prepares us for the weight of the purpose we will carry. And ultimately, Joseph's purpose far outweighed the turmoil he endured to discover it. The same is true for you. Because in God's hands, what the Enemy meant for evil becomes the very tool God uses to bring forth purpose, provision, and breakthrough, not just for us, but for others connected to our assignment.

Isaiah 64:8 declares, "Yet you, Lord, are our Father. We are the clay, you are the potter; we are all the work of your hand." *The* imagery is clear—God is the Master Potter, and we are the clay. Becoming requires more than desire; it requires surrender. Clay doesn't argue with the potter. It doesn't dictate the design or resist the reshaping. It yields, fully trusting the potter's pressure, pace, and precision.

Sometimes, that shaping hurts. The wheel spins. The pressure intensifies. Cracks begin to form. And in some seasons, the Potter must even crush the form to remake the vessel. But He never does so out of cruelty—only out of care. He sees what we cannot. He knows what we're called to carry, and He lovingly prepares us to hold it well.

Often, the process is lonely. But loneliness is not evidence of God's absence. It is often the environment of His most intimate work. He separates us not to isolate us, but to consecrate us. He silences the noise so His voice can be heard more clearly.

Think of Moses in the desert. Stripped of privilege, position, and power, he was hidden for forty years—tending sheep on the backside of the wilderness. But it was there, in the solitude, that God ignited a burning bush encounter. It was in isolation that Moses received his call and was prepared to lead a nation. His desert wasn't punishment; it was preparation. It wasn't a delay; it was divine alignment.

Let this truth settle in your spirit: isolation is not abandonment. It is alignment. When God pulls you back, it's only to launch you forward. When He slows you down, it's only to sharpen your discernment. When He hides you, it's to heal you. The silence of the process is where revelation is born.

So, if you find yourself in a season that feels slow, hidden, or hard, don't resist it. Don't despise it. God is working. He is molding. He is preparing. And when He's finished, you won't just be ready for purpose; you'll be refined for His glory.

Hidden Before Honored

There are people who desire the platform before the process. They want the reward without the refinement, the influence without the inner work. But in the economy of God's kingdom, elevation follows preparation. Honor follows hiddenness. Before God reveals what, He's building, He often conceals what He's forming.

David is a perfect example. In 1 Samuel 16, he was anointed king while still a teenage shepherd—young, unnoticed, and seemingly unqualified. He wasn't paraded in front of Israel. He wasn't immediately handed a crown. Instead, he returned to the pasture. Why? Because God knew the pasture was where David's heart would be shaped for the throne he would one day occupy.

The pasture is God's classroom. It's where character is cultivated, pride is pruned, and humility is planted. It's where we learn to serve without applause, to worship without a crowd, and to obey without validation. It is in those hidden places that God prepares us to carry His glory with integrity and to handle the weight of leadership with wisdom.

Becoming rarely happens in the spotlight. It unfolds in obscurity—when no one is watching, when affirmation is scarce, and when recognition is delayed. But that doesn't mean the process is insignificant. In fact, it's often essential.

Galatians 6:9 encourages us, "Let us not grow weary in well doing: for in due season we shall reap, if we faint not." The process of becoming can be exhausting. It stretches our faith, challenges our comfort, and demands our perseverance. But it is never in vain. Every obedient step, every hidden act of faithfulness,

47

every quiet sacrifice is seen by God, and it all counts. There is a *due season*, and it belongs to those who refuse to quit. The harvest of your purpose is directly tied to the seed of your endurance. That's why you cannot afford to despise the process. And you certainly can't afford to rush it.

Don't forfeit your future by trying to bypass the very season God is using to build you. What feels like delay is often divine design. What looks like being overlooked may actually be God covering you until your character can carry what your calling requires.

You're not being ignored. You're being incubated. You're not stuck. You're being *stabilized*. So embrace the pasture. Honor the hidden place. Because those who are faithful in obscurity are the ones God can trust with visibility.

In God's timing, you won't just step into purpose—you'll be *ready* for it.

From Process to Power

If the hidden place is where we are formed, then the pressure place is where we are forged. God never wastes our pain. He uses it as preparation for power. The very process that humbles us is the one that strengthens us. Becoming is not simply about getting through trials; it's about *gaining* what you need in the fire to stand when you're called.

Pressure is part of the path. Just ask Joseph, Esther, Moses, or David. Every person in Scripture who walked in divine authority first had to walk through divine refinement. Why? Because God is more concerned with *who you are becoming* than where you are going. He knows that spiritual authority without spiritual maturity leads to collapse. But when you are forged in the fire, your faith is not just emotional; it's enduring.

Romans 5:3-4 reminds us: "We also glory in our sufferings, because we know that suffering produces perseverance; perseverance, character; and character, hope."

This is the divine order. Pressure produces perseverance. Perseverance builds character. Character gives birth to hope. And hope anchors your power in something deeper than platforms—it anchors it in purpose.

There is a power that doesn't come from charisma; it comes from crucifixion. Dying to self. Dying to pride. Dying to timelines and personal agendas. And it is in *that* death that resurrection power lives.

Think of Jesus. Before resurrection came Gethsemane. Before power was displayed, pressure was endured. The garden was the place where He chose obedience in the face of agony. And that obedience released the greatest outpouring of power the world has ever known.

In your becoming season, don't run from pressure. Let it press you *into* God, not away from Him. Let it sharpen your ears to His voice, strengthen your resolve to obey, and prepare your spirit to carry what He has placed inside you.

You don't need to manufacture your power. You don't have to prove yourself. All you have to do is remain surrendered. The process is producing something you can't yet see—strength, depth, resilience, discernment, authority.

God is not just trying to *get you through* this season. He's trying to *grow you through* it.

Delayed Doesn't Mean Denied

Too many times, we mistake the delays of God for the denial of His promises. But delay is not denial; it's often divine development. Just because it hasn't been fulfilled *yet* doesn't mean it won't. God often reveals the vision first, then leads us into a season of formation to prepare us for the weight of what He has promised.

Ask Abraham. When God told him that his descendants would outnumber the stars in the sky (Genesis 15:5), Abraham didn't hold a newborn the next morning. He waited decades for Isaac to arrive. And just when hope seemed too far gone, when his body was old and Sarah's womb was barren, God reaffirmed the promise. In fact, when the angel appeared again and declared that the promise would come to pass, Sarah laughed (Genesis 18:12)—not out of joy, but disbelief.

Her laughter was rooted in the impossibility of her circumstance. But God had the final say.

"Is anything too hard for the Lord?" the angel asked (Genesis 18:14). That question still echoes today. God specializes in fulfilling promises long after others have written them off.

And our greatest example? Look to Jesus. Though He was the Son of God, full of power and purpose, He didn't begin His earthly ministry until the age of thirty. For thirty hidden years, the Savior of the world lived in obscurity—waiting, growing, and walking in obedience. Then, in only three years, He fulfilled His assignment and changed the course of human history.

Why the wait? Because divine timing is never rushed. God is not just interested in what you're called to do. He's deeply invested in who you are when you do it.

So, if you're in a waiting season, take heart. The pause doesn't mean God has forgotten. It means He's preparing. He's refining your faith, strengthening your character, and aligning every piece of your life for the appointed time.

God isn't in a rush—He's
in a refining.

Lessons in the Becoming Season

1. Obedience precedes opportunity — God will test your faithfulness in private before He promotes you in public.

2. Character must match calling — The process works out the kinks in your heart that would otherwise sabotage your destiny.

3. Faith is forged in the fire — Trials refine your trust in God. You come out wiser, stronger, and more surrendered.

4. Growth often looks like grief — You have to let go of who you are to become who you're called to be. It's okay to grieve old versions of yourself.

5. Second Corinthians 4:17 says, "For our light affliction, which is but for a moment, works for us a far more exceeding and eternal weight of glory." The process is working *for*

you, not against you. Even in the stretching, God is shaping your soul to sustain the weight of your assignment.

6. Becoming is not just about doing—it's about being. It's about becoming like Christ. Before you can lead like Him, speak like Him, or serve like Him, you must *become* like Him. Romans 8:29 reminds us that we are "predestined to be conformed to the image of His Son."

Becoming requires a surrendered heart and a willing spirit. It asks the question: *Will you let God make you before He makes you known?* Because if He reveals you before you're ready, the weight of visibility will crush what your character can't carry.

So, embrace the season. Let God shape you, stretch you, and strip away what no longer serves your assignment. Because when becoming meets belief, a breakthrough is inevitable.

Reflection Questions

- What season of "becoming" are you currently in?

- In what ways have you seen God shaping you through pressure or pain?
- What parts of you still resist the Potter's hand?
- How can you shift your mindset from frustration to formation?
- What would it look like for you to fully embrace this process?

Let's Pray!

Most gracious and eternal God, our Father, thank You for not rushing my process, even though it was difficult to be patient. And when I don't understand the season I'm in, I trust that You are shaping me for purpose. Help me to yield to Your hands. Teach me to find peace in the becoming. Strip away what is not of You and strengthen what is. May I be conformed to the image of Your Son. I surrender to Your process—use it to prepare me for what You've prepared for me. In Jesus' name. Amen.

CHAPTER 4

On Display: When Purpose Goes Public

There comes a time when what God has been doing in you begins to emerge through you. This is the moment when purpose steps out of the shadows and into the spotlight—not for show, but for service. When your life goes on display, it becomes a visible testimony of God's grace, power, and intention. But make no mistake: visibility is not about vanity. It is about *stewardship*. It's about honoring the responsibility that comes with being seen.

Matthew 5:14-16 captures this perfectly: "You are the light of the world. A town built on a hill cannot be hidden... let your light shine before others, that they may see your good deeds and glorify your Father in heaven." God doesn't put you on display, so people can praise *you,* but for them to see *Him* through you.

Purpose attracts attention—and with attention comes accountability. The higher God elevates you, the deeper your roots must grow. This is why the process of becoming is so vital before going public. Influence without integrity is a setup for a fall.

Platform Requires Stewardship

God doesn't elevate us to entertain. He elevates us to impact. Whether your platform is a pulpit, a podcast, a classroom, or a kitchen table, the assignment remains the same: reflect Christ.

In Luke 12:48, Jesus reminds us, "To whom much is given, much will be required."

When purpose goes public:
- Your influence increases, but so does your responsibility.
- Your voice gets louder, but your heart must stay humble.

- Your reach grows wider, but your roots must grow deeper.

Your life becomes a mirror.

When people look at your life, what do they see reflected? The apostle Paul said in 1 Corinthians 11:1, "Follow me as I follow Christ." That is the ultimate goal of purpose in public—to live in such a way that others are drawn to your *Savior*, not your platform.

When God Reveals You, Protect the Glory

In Acts 12:21-23, King Herod gave a public address and received glory from the people. Because he did not give glory to God, judgment followed. It's a sobering reminder: when God puts you on display, He still deserves the glory.

Being on display doesn't mean you're perfect; it means you're available. It means you've accepted the mantle and are committed to carrying it with humility and faithfulness. People may applaud the visible fruit, but only God sees the hidden roots.

God Displays What He Can Trust

Before God puts you on display, He puts you through testing. He examines the heart. He checks the motives. He's not looking for performers. He's looking for stewards. And when your private obedience aligns with your public expression, He can trust you with visibility.

Scriptures to Anchor Your Visibility

- Trust God to guide your visibility and direct your path (Proverbs 3:5-6).
- "He must become greater; I must become less" (John 3:30).
- Use your gifts to serve others, faithfully administering God's grace (1 Peter 4:10).

Reflection Questions

- What has God entrusted you to display in this season?
- Are you more focused on being seen or being faithful?
- How can you steward your influence in a way that brings glory to God?
- What habits or practices will keep you grounded as God expands your visibility?

- In what ways can you reflect Christ more clearly to those who see you?

Let's Pray!

Heavenly Father, I thank You for trusting me with visibility. Help me to carry it with humility, steward it with wisdom, and reflect You in everything I say and do. Keep my heart anchored in Your truth, my motives pure, and my platform centered on Christ. Let my life be a light that points others to You. When people look at me, may they see You.

CHAPTER 5

Responding vs. Reacting Living with Discernment and Discipline

In my world, there's a clear difference between reacting and responding. Reactions are emotional, impulsive, and often misaligned with God's will. Responses, on the other hand, are intentional, Spirit-led, and rooted in wisdom.

Living out loud on purpose requires discernment, which comes through relationship with the Holy Spirit. Jesus said in John 16:13, "But when He, the Spirit of truth, comes, He will guide you into all the truth."

The Holy Spirit empowers us to pause, reflect, and respond in alignment with God's purpose, rather than react in ways that sabotage it.

Stephen Covey once said, "Responsibility is the ability to respond." That powerful truth calls us back to intentional living. It reminds us that maturity isn't measured by the absence of hardship, but by how we handle what life throws our way. We may not control the challenges, but we do choose our posture.

Joshua's Response

Joshua declared in Joshua 24:15, "Choose this day whom you will serve... But as for me and my house, we will serve the Lord." This wasn't a passive statement; it was a bold, public declaration rooted in conviction. Joshua made a decision—not just to live intentionally, but to live responsibly. He understood that his leadership required clarity, and his legacy demanded commitment. His response wasn't shaped by the shifting opinions of the crowd or the uncertainty of the future. He didn't react to fear or cultural pressure as we often do today, but he responded to God's faithfulness.

Joshua saw firsthand how emotional reactions led Israel astray—how murmuring, fear, and rebellion delayed their promise. So, when it was time to make a choice, he responded from a place of spiritual maturity. He wasn't driven by his emotion; he was guided by revelation. His decision reflected a heart anchored in covenant, not convenience. In that moment, Joshua modeled what it looks like to walk in discernment and discipline—to respond with purpose rather than react out of pressure.

His words still echo today: *Choose this day.* Every day presents us with the opportunity to react according to the flesh or respond according to the Spirit. Joshua's life reminds us that godly leadership begins with godly choices—deliberate, Spirit-led responses that shape not only our lives but the generations that follow.

Reacting Can Ruin Purpose

When we react impulsively—whether in anger, fear, or offense—we open the door for the Enemy to derail our destiny. Reactions are rooted in the flesh; responses are rooted in the Spirit.

Living out loud on purpose means recognizing the weight of our decisions and allowing God to filter our emotions before they become actions.

Through the Holy Spirit, we have the power to choose our actions. Proverbs 15:1 teaches, "A gentle answer turns away wrath, but a harsh word stirs up anger." In moments of pressure, we must pause and invite the Holy Spirit to guide our words and actions. Purpose is too precious to be poisoned by an unfiltered reaction.

Choosing Response over Reactions

The fruit of the Spirit is self-control. Paul writes in Galatians 5:22-23, "But the fruit of the Spirit is love, joy, peace, patience, kindness, goodness, faithfulness, gentleness, *self-control*. Against such things there is no law."

Self-control is not just about restraint; it's about reliance. It's not manufactured through willpower; it's cultivated through intimacy with the Holy Spirit. This fruit allows us to master our impulses instead of being mastered by them. It is the evidence of a Spirit-led life and the safeguard of purposeful living.

When you're faced with a moment that would typically trigger a reaction, it's self-control that invites you to *respond* instead. Self-control puts a leash on the tongue, a guard on the heart, and a check on the emotions. It allows us to be slow to speak, slow to anger, and quick to listen because the Spirit is governing, not the flesh. When the Spirit is in control, so are you.

God Is Our Anchor

Psalm 46:1 says, "God is our refuge and strength, a very present help in trouble." When we lean into God in challenging moments, we receive the strength to respond with grace. We're reminded that the battle isn't ours—it belongs to the Lord.

When you're grounded in God, there's no need to prove yourself. You simply need to be who He called you to be.

Here are some keys to responding instead of reacting:

Pause and Pray

Pause and pray before speaking or acting. Why is this important? In a world that celebrates quick responses and instant reactions, pausing to pray can feel countercultural—but it is profoundly powerful. Taking a moment to pause gives the Holy Spirit room to guide your thoughts, calm your emotions, and align your response with God's will rather than your own impulses. When we pause, we create space between stimulus and response. That space is where wisdom lives. It's where rash words are replaced with grace, anger is softened by discernment, and fear is met with faith. Pausing interrupts the cycle of reaction and makes room for a response that is measured, meaningful, and Spirit-led.

Prayer in that pause connects you to the source of clarity and truth. It reminds you that you are not alone—that God is present, and He sees the whole picture, even when you don't. Whether you're facing a difficult conversation, a big decision, or a moment of temptation, prayer invites God into the situation and shifts the outcome.

Jesus Himself modeled this. Before choosing His disciples, performing miracles, and facing the cross, He paused and prayed. If the Son of God needed to pause and pray, how much more do we?

Pausing and praying protects relationships, guards your peace, and preserves your witness. It ensures your words build and not break, and your actions reflect Christ, not your flesh.

In short, pausing and praying positions you to respond not from emotion but from purpose.

Seek Wisdom from the Word, Not Just Your Feelings – Why This Matters

I'll be the first to admit—feelings are real, but they're not always reliable. They fluctuate with circumstances, shift with moods, and are often influenced by fear, fatigue, or frustration. While emotions are part of our God-given design and can serve as helpful indicators, they were never meant to sit in the driver's seat of our decisions. That's why we must anchor ourselves in the unchanging truth of God's Word. The Bible is more than a book of encouragement. It's a wellspring of wisdom. It offers timeless principles, divine direction, and spiritual discernment for every situation we face. When emotions are high and clarity seems distant, the Word becomes a steady compass, guiding us back to God's heart and will.

Proverbs 3:5-6 reminds us to "lean not on our own understanding," which includes the limited lens of our feelings. God's wisdom transcends what we can see or sense in the moment. When we choose to seek His truth in Scripture, we invite Him to lead us by eternal truth.

This kind of wisdom guards us from impulsive decisions and regretful words. It enables us to respond with grace, patience, and courage—even when our emotions urge us otherwise. It empowers us to choose faith over fear, forgiveness over offense, and peace over panic.

Ultimately, seeking wisdom from the Word builds a life grounded in discernment and direction, not emotional chaos. It deepens our spiritual maturity and anchors us in God's voice above our own impulses.

Surround Yourself with Spirit-Filled Counsel – Why This Is Essential

"Without counsel purposes are disappointed: but in the multitude of counsellors they are established" (Proverbs 15:22).

The people you allow to speak into your life can either sharpen your purpose or sabotage it. That's why it's crucial to surround yourself with counsel that is not only wise but Spirit-filled. You need voices that are led by God, rooted in His Word, and sensitive to His voice. Good intentions aren't enough; you need godly insight.

Spirit-filled counsel offers more than advice; it brings alignment. These are people who pray before they speak, who discern beyond the surface, and who point you back to God rather than their own opinions. They don't simply echo your feelings—they challenge your faith. They help you filter your desires through the lens of God's truth, not just your emotions or cultural norms.

Proverbs 15:22 reminds us that our plans are more likely to succeed when guided by wise counsel. This means inviting voices into your life who will hold you accountable, speak truth in love, and remind you of what God has said, especially when your own vision feels cloudy. These are the people who will pray with you, fast with you, and walk beside you through seasons of uncertainty.

Surrounding yourself with Spirit-filled counsel isn't a sign of weakness—it's a mark of spiritual maturity. Even Jesus had an inner circle. If the Son of God valued aligned, intentional relationships, so should we. God often speaks through His people, so who you allow close to you matters. Choose those who build your faith, guard your growth, and support your God-given assignment.

Ask the Holy Spirit to Lead You in Real Time

God never intended for us to navigate life on our own. In John 14:26, Jesus said the Holy Spirit would be our Helper, Teacher, and Guide. He's not just a distant presence reserved for church services or quiet time. He is your constant companion, available to lead you moment by moment.

Asking the Holy Spirit to lead you in real time means cultivating a continual awareness of His presence. It's not just about the big, life-changing decisions—though He certainly helps with those. It's about inviting Him into the everyday: what to say in a hard conversation, how to respond to a frustrating email, whether to speak or stay silent, or even how to spend your time. His leadership is practical, personal, and precise.

When you ask the Holy Spirit to lead you in real time, you're acknowledging your dependence on God. You're surrendering your natural instincts in exchange for supernatural insight. He sees what you can't. He knows what's ahead, what's behind, and what's hidden in the hearts of others. His prompting may come as a gentle nudge, a pause in your spirit, a sudden clarity, or a wave of unexpected peace.

Spirit-led living is not about perfection. It is about posture, a posture of listening, yielding, and responding. It develops as you grow in sensitivity and obedience. The more you ask, the more you recognize His voice. The more you follow, the more confident you become in His leadership.

Ultimately, real-time guidance from the Holy Spirit leads to peace, power, and purpose. It allows you to live in sync with heaven, even when the world around you is chaotic. It transforms ordinary moments into divine appointments.

So ask Him. Then listen, trust, and follow. Even if it doesn't make sense right away. The Holy Spirit never leads you wrong.

Refuse to be Baited by Offense or Provocation

This is absolutely essential because it's a trap designed to distract, divide, and derail your purpose.

Offense is one of the Enemy's most subtle and effective strategies. It doesn't always arrive through outright conflict. More often, it slips in quietly: through a careless comment, a perceived slight, or unmet expectations. Provocation can creep in through criticism, betrayal, or even a simple misunderstanding. And if we're not careful, we take the bait—responding in anger, retreating in silence, or harboring resentment.

Offense is more than a feeling; it's a spiritual snare. It tempts you to pick up what God already told you to lay down: bitterness, pride, unforgiveness. The Enemy knows that a wounded heart leads to a distracted mind—and a distracted mind quickly becomes a misaligned life. When you're offended, your focus shifts from your assignment to the insult.

Refusing the bait of offense isn't weakness; it's wisdom. It's choosing maturity over reaction. It's deciding that your peace is more valuable than proving a point. It's recognizing that your purpose is too great to be tangled in petty battles or personal vendettas.

When Jesus was provoked, He didn't retaliate. He responded with silence, wisdom, or grace. That's power under control.

Proverbs 19:11 says, "A person's wisdom yields patience; it is to one's glory to overlook an offense." Overlooking doesn't mean pretending it didn't hurt—it means refusing to let it take root. It means trusting God to handle what your pride wants to confront. It means keeping your heart clean so your spirit can remain free. Every offense is an opportunity: to react in the flesh or respond by the Spirit. Choose wisely. Refuse the bait. Protect your peace. Guard your growth.

James 1:19 gives us the blueprint: "Everyone should be quick to listen, slow to speak and slow to become angry." This is the posture of the purposeful. When we live out loud, people are watching—not to see perfection, but to see authenticity. Responding with love, truth, and wisdom puts the glory of God on display. It reveals a life surrendered—not to impulse, but to divine purpose.

Reflection Questions

- Do you tend to react or respond when you are under pressure?
- What situations have revealed your need for more Spirit-led responses?
- How can you invite the Holy Spirit into your daily decision-making?
- What truths from God's Word can anchor your emotions?
- What does it mean for you to live responsibly in this season?

Let's Pray!

Holy Spirit, please help me to respond rather than react. Through Your precious Holy Spirit, remind me that it is *You* who empowers me to walk in the fruit of the Spirit, especially self-control. Teach me to pause, listen, and lean on Your wisdom. I surrender my emotions to You and ask for discernment in every moment. Let my words be seasoned with grace and my actions guided by purpose. May I live as one who chooses responsibility and reflects Your love in all I do. In Jesus' name. Amen.

CHAPTER 6

Identity: Remember Who You Are

In the previous chapter, we focused on responding versus reacting. We recognized that being empowered by the Holy Spirit gives us the ability to respond to life's circumstances. But living out loud also comes with its caveats. We will further explore these challenges and complexities later in the book. For now, one of the challenges you will face when discovering your purpose is remembering who you are. Why is this important when living out loud? You can't live out loud if you don't know who is talking.

I must admit that I have struggled countless times to understand my purpose. For much of my life, I was the daughter of, the sister of, or the wife of. For years,

I hid in the shadows, comfortable with not having fully discovered or secured my own destiny. But something shifted! God began to stir something in me that I could not ignore.

I started to sense there was more—more to say, more to give, more to be. The same God who had watched me shrink back was now calling me to rise. He wasn't asking me to deny who I had been, but to discover who I truly am in Him.

It wasn't a loud moment at first, but it was a decisive one. I committed to stop living quietly behind titles and roles and to start living *boldly* and *intentionally*, *on purpose*. I realized my voice had value. My story carried weight. And my life—yes, even mine—was meant to be lived out loud, for God's glory.

As always, the Lord reminded me: "Before I formed you in the womb I knew you, before you were born I set you apart" (Jeremiah 1:5a).

That verse echoed in my heart, reminding me that my voice matters, not because it's perfect, but because it's *purposed*. So, I chose to live out loud, on purpose.

This speaks to the heart of identity. Before you can embrace your purpose, before you can walk in your calling, before you can stand in authority, you must first know who you are. And even more importantly, you must know *whose you are.*

The world will undoubtedly try to define you by your past, pain, performance, or popularity. But none of those things reflect your true identity. As a child of God, your identity is found in Christ.

Ephesians 2:10 declares, "For we are God's masterpiece. He has created us anew in Christ Jesus, so we can do the good things He planned for us long ago." You are not a mistake. You are not an afterthought. You are a masterpiece—designed with divine intention and purpose.

First Peter 2:9 reminds us, "But you are a chosen people, a royal priesthood, a holy nation, God's special possession, that you may declare the praises of

Him who called you out of darkness into His wonderful light."

Your identity carries value, purpose, and spiritual authority. You've been called out of something, so you can fully live *into* something greater.

Galatians 2:20 says, "I have been crucified with Christ and I no longer live, but Christ lives in me. The life I now live in the body, I live by faith in the Son of God, who loved me and gave Himself for me." This verse reminds us that our identity is not self-made—it's Christ-formed. We no longer live according to our own definitions or the world's standards. We live by faith, under the covering of grace, and through the lens of God's love.

Identity Is the Foundation of Purpose

If you don't know who you are, you won't know what to do because identity answers the questions of origin, value, and direction. Why is that important?

At its core, identity is not just about who we are. It's about whose we are, where we come from, and where we're going. It is the foundational lens through which we view ourselves and interpret the world around us. When we understand our God-given identity, we begin to uncover the answers to three of life's most pressing questions:

1. Origin – Where Did I Come From?

Identity reminds us that we are not cosmic accidents or random outcomes of chance. We were created intentionally by a God who knew us *before* we were formed in our mothers' wombs (Jeremiah 1:5). Our origin is divine, not coincidental. We are the handiwork of the Creator, crafted in His image with purpose in mind.

2. Value – What Am I Worth?

Our identity reveals our immeasurable worth. Not because of titles, talents, or accomplishments, but because we bear the fingerprint of God. We were bought with a price—the precious blood of Jesus—and that alone settles the question of value. Knowing our identity silences the lies that say we're not enough and reminds us that we are deeply loved, chosen, and significant.

3. Direction – Where Am I Going?

When you know who you are and whose you are, you gain clarity about where you're headed. Identity gives purpose its footing. It aligns our steps with God's divine plan and positions us to walk confidently into our future. This is why Jeremiah 29:11 is so powerful—it reveals that our direction is not random, but part of a hope-filled, God-authored journey.

When we live out loud on purpose, it begins with embracing our identity. You cannot live boldly, speak truthfully, or serve meaningfully if you are unclear about who you are. Identity is the anchor that grounds us, the compass that guides us, and the fuel that drives us forward.

When you remember that you are a child of God, created in His image, redeemed by His blood, and filled with His Spirit, you begin to live with the confidence and clarity that purpose demands.

Jesus Modeled Secure Identity

Even Jesus, before beginning His public ministry, received affirmation from the Father: "This is my beloved Son, in whom I am well pleased" (Matthew

3:17). He didn't perform miracles to earn that affirmation—He received it before He did a thing. That's
the power of identity: it secures you before success,
struggle, and public recognition. If Jesus needed that
foundation, how much more do we?

Rejecting False Labels

So many of us walk around wearing labels God never
gave us—labels shaped by trauma, fear, rejection, or
shame. But living out loud on purpose means remov-
ing those false labels and replacing them with the
truth of God's Word.

- The world may call you broken—God calls
  you whole.
- The Enemy may call you worthless—God
  calls you chosen.
- People may call you forgotten—God calls
  you His.
- Your past may say you're disqualified—God
  says you're called.

When you accept God's identity for your life, you
stop living for approval and start living from approval. You live anchored, not anxious. Grounded,

not grasping.

Living Authentically

To remember who you are is to live from your spiritual DNA. It is to live without apology, pretense, and fear. You no longer have to hustle for validation or compete for affirmation. When you know who you are, you walk in peace, power, and purpose. Authenticity becomes your norm, not your exception. You stop shrinking to fit in, and you start standing to stand out—for the glory of God.

You, too, can walk in your God-given identity. Here's how:

1. Renew your mind daily with the truth of God's Word (Romans 12:2).
2. Speak life over yourself, declarations rooted in Scripture.
3. Surround yourself with an identity-affirming community
4. Let go of old mindsets that no longer serve your calling.
5. Ask the Holy Spirit to constantly remind you of who you are in Christ.
6. Celebrate progress over perfection; you're

becoming more of who you already are in
Him

Reflection Questions

- What labels are you still wearing that God
  never gave you?
- How can you root your identity more
  deeply in Christ?
- What does it look like for you to live authentically?
- Who has God called you to be that you
  have been afraid to embrace?
- How can you encourage others to remember who they are?

Let's Pray!

Most gracious and Eternal God, thank You for creating me with intention and calling me by name. I re-
nounce every false label and declare that my identity
is found in Christ alone. Help me to live boldly, authentically, and securely in who You say I am. Let
my life reflect Your truth and bring glory to Your
name. In Jesus' name. Amen.

CHAPTER 7

Voice: You Were Never Meant to Be Silent

As you begin to understand that purpose begins with discovering identity, another truth should also emerge: you were never meant to be silent. Frankly speaking, I believe it is nearly impossible to stifle a voice that truly knows who it is and why it exists. Your voice is a weapon, a witness, and a vessel of purpose.

One of the greatest lies the Enemy uses to paralyze purpose is silence. If he can convince you that your voice doesn't matter, he can rob you of the authority that comes with identity. Silence is his strategy. A silenced voice often leads to a stagnated purpose.

Jesus warns us plainly in John 10:10, "The thief cometh not, but for to steal, and to kill, and to destroy." The Enemy's objective is clear: steal your identity, kill your confidence, and destroy your destiny. And silencing your voice is a tactical move to keep your purpose dormant, so that you remain powerless. But make no mistake: God didn't give you revelation so you can stay quiet. That's why we never end with the Enemy's plan. We speak the words of Jesus with boldness: "I am come that they might have life, and that they might have it more abundantly."

The word "abundantly" is translated from the Greek word *perissos* (περισσὸν), meaning exceeding some number or measure, over and above, more than necessary, superabundant, superior, or extraordinary. Shall I go on? Let me end with this one, surpassing uncommon and beyond expectation. By now, you should be exploding with purpose.

Abundant life is not quiet; it's highly expressive and liberating. Jesus has given you more than enough to live purposefully. In fact, He has already surpassed the supply of what you need to live out loud for Him.

Living abundantly is a declaration that you know who you are, why you're here, and who sent you. It is the fulfillment of identity, the fuel of purpose, and the freedom to walk boldly in your God-given assignment.

So when Jesus promises abundant life, He's extending an invitation—not just to breathe, but to *be*. Not just to exist, but to express. That is the heart of living out loud—on purpose. Jesus gave you your voice so you could proclaim it.

The Bible declares in Proverbs 18:21, "Death and life are in the power of the tongue: and they that love it shall eat the fruit thereof." Your voice carries weight. It creates. It shapes. It builds up—or tears down. When you live out loud on purpose, you embrace the responsibility of using your voice for expression and impact.

Your voice doesn't have to be the loudest in the room to be powerful, but it does have to be present. God has placed something unique inside of you—truth, wisdom, experience, testimony—and He expects you to release it for His glory. Silence might feel safe, but it's not where transformation lives.

Speaking with Authority

To speak with authority doesn't mean to be loud—it means to be rooted. It means knowing you carry the Spirit of the living God within you. And when you speak His truth, mountains move, chains break, and atmospheres shift. Jesus didn't waste words. He used them. And every time He spoke, things changed.

We are called to walk in that same authority through the Holy Spirit. Acts 4:31 declares, "And when they had prayed, the place was shaken where they were assembled together; and they were all filled with the Holy Ghost, and they spake the word of God with boldness."

That kind of boldness didn't come from personality—it came from presence. The Holy Spirit empowers you to speak with clarity, truth, and power.

Your Story Matters

Your voice carries your story. And your story—redeemed, transformed, and still unfolding—is living evidence of God's goodness.

Revelation 12:11 says, "And they overcame him by the blood of the Lamb, and by the word of their testimony."

Your voice is how you testify. Your voice is how you give hell a headache and give others hope. We often underestimate the power of our personal stories. We think, "Who would listen to me?" But someone needs to hear exactly what you've come through.

Your voice is a bridge to someone else's breakthrough.

Don't Let Fear Muzzle Your Message

One of the attributes of fear is intimidation. Fear will try to silence you. Shame will try to mute your purpose. But God has not given you a spirit of fear. Second Timothy 1:7 reminds us: "For God has not given us a spirit of fear, but of power and of love and of a sound mind."

You don't have to speak perfectly—you just have to speak faithfully. You must recognize that when fear is present, the presence and power of God cannot fully operate. Why? Because fear doesn't come from God. God didn't give you fear—He gave you power. So turn up the volume. Speak!

Yes, there will always be reasons to stay silent—criticism, insecurity, doubt. But there's a greater reason to speak: obedience. When you release what God has placed in your spirit, you align yourself with heaven's assignment. Don't wait until you feel "ready." Speak anyway. Speaking is more than just making a declaration. It's about speaking up and speaking out.

When You Speak, Things Shift

- You speak truth that confronts every lie.
- You speak hope that disrupts despair.
- You speak life that revives what's been dead.
- You speak love that heals broken hearts.

Whether you're leading a meeting, teaching a class, praying with a friend, or speaking from a stage, every moment is an opportunity to use your voice with purpose.

Practical Ways to Use Your Voice

- Declare Scripture out loud — faith comes by hearing.
- Encourage others — your words could be someone's lifeline.
- Pray boldly — take authority in your intercession.
- Speak up for justice — advocate for those without a voice.
- Teach and lead — share what God has taught you.
- Share your testimony — let your past point someone to Christ.

Reflection Questions

- Where have you allowed fear to silence your voice?
- What truth has God placed within you that you need to proclaim?
- How can you use your voice to edify and uplift others?
- What lies do you need to confront with the truth of God's Word?
- How has your story been shaped to benefit

someone else?

Let's Pray!

Most Gracious and Eternal God, thank You for giving me a voice. Forgive me for the times I've stayed silent when You called me to speak and I allowed fear to take the reigns. Embolden me by Your Spirit to speak with truth, love, and clarity. Use my voice to bring healing, deliverance, and hope to those around me. Let everything I say be rooted in Your Word and led by Your Spirit. Let me speak with power but walk in humility. In Jesus' name.

CHAPTER 8

Fireproof: Standing When It's Hard

Remember those caveats I mentioned earlier in Chapter 4? Living out loud on purpose is powerful, but let's be honest, it's not always easy. Purpose comes with pressure. If you're going to stand for something, you have to be prepared for what may rise up against you. Because purpose doesn't just shine in places of comfort; it's proven in the fire. And here's the beauty of it: God doesn't just put you on display—He preserves you in the process.

Sometimes the greatest evidence of your purpose isn't the applause you receive, but the pressure you endure. Pressure doesn't mean God's absence—it often signals His presence. When the fire comes, it's usually a sign that the anointing is near, the breakthrough is close, and the Enemy is threatened. But hear this: the fire is not your end—it's your refining ground.

Daniel Chapter 3 tells the story of three young men, Shadrach, Meshach, and Abednego, who refused to bow to a golden image, even under threat of death. They chose obedience over acceptance, conviction over compromise. Their stand led them to the furnace, but their faith led them through it. And when they came out, not only were they unharmed, but they also didn't even smell like smoke.

That's what God does. He doesn't always take the heat away, but He walks with you through it. In fact, it's in the fire that you discover what's really inside of you, and more importantly, who is standing beside you.

James 1:2-4 urges us: "Count it all joy when ye fall into divers temptations; knowing this, that the trying of your faith worketh patience. But let patience have her perfect work, that ye may be perfect and entire, wanting nothing."

Your trials don't mean you're off track; they often mean you're right on it. The test is evidence that you're carrying something worth attacking.

When you live out loud, expect resistance. But also expect reinforcement because God isn't just calling you to stand—He's giving you the strength to do it. He provides the grace to endure, the peace to sustain, and the wisdom to keep moving forward.

Second Corinthians 4:8-9 says, "We are hard pressed on every side, but not crushed; perplexed, but not in despair; persecuted, but not abandoned; struck down, but not destroyed." The fire may be hot, but your faith is fireproof. God doesn't allow the fire to consume you. He uses it to consecrate you.

Why the Fire Is Necessary

Just as gold is heated until impurities rise to the surface and are removed, the fire of trials reveals what's hidden within us—our fears, attitudes, motives, and weaknesses. The process may be uncomfortable, but it's necessary for transformation. The fire strips away pride, complacency, and compromise. In its place, God cultivates humility, perseverance, and integrity. What emerges is a more authentic, Christlike version of you.

The fire doesn't destroy—it defines. It confirms your convictions. You learn what you truly believe when tested. Convictions aren't solidified in comfort; they're proven in crisis.

It's easy to declare your faith when everything is going well, but the fire forces you to confront whether your beliefs are truly rooted in God or in your circumstances.

When tested, you discover the depth of your spiritual foundation.

- Do you believe God is good—even when you don't see good?
- Do you trust His plan—even when you don't understand it?

The fire distinguishes shallow belief from unwavering faith. It reveals if your "yes" to God is conditional or committed.

It reveals God's power — others see the miracle in your stand. Your endurance in the fire becomes a platform for God's glory. When others watch you walk through intense difficulty yet remain faithful, peaceful, and hopeful, they witness something supernatural. They begin to see that it's not your strength carrying you—it's God's. Just as Nebuchadnezzar saw a fourth man in the fire with the Hebrew boys, people will see evidence of divine presence in your trial. Your testimony in the fire becomes a light that leads others to Christ.

It releases promotion — after the fire, God elevated the Hebrew boys to new levels of influence. The fire is often the final test before elevation. For Shadrach, Meshach, and Abednego, their refusal to bow—and their faithfulness in the furnace—resulted in public recognition and divine promotion. God used the fire not only to prepare them internally, but also to position them externally. When you remain faithful under pressure, God can trust you with greater responsibility, deeper purpose, and higher platforms. Your fiery trial becomes the gateway to your next season of favor and influence.

It deepens your trust — you learn that God is not just a deliverer; He is a sustainer. Sometimes God doesn't immediately remove the fire; instead, He walks with you through it. And in that sustained presence, you discover a deeper dimension of who He is. He is not just the One who brings you out—He's the One who keeps you while you're in it. You begin to trust Him not just for the outcome, but in the process. This kind of trust isn't built in the absence of fire. It's forged in the heat of it when you have nothing left to hold on to but Him, and you find that He is enough.

Standing When It's Hard Looks Like:

- Refusing to compromise even when it's inconvenient
- Choosing truth over popularity
- Remaining faithful when prayers seem unanswered
- Holding on to hope when the fire gets hotter
- Praising God in the midst of pain

- Speaking life when all you see is loss

You Are Not Alone in the Fire

The most powerful part of the story in Daniel Chapter 3 is this: when the king looked into the flames, he saw *four* men, not three. And the fourth looked like "a Son of God." This scripture reaffirms that Jesus was in the fire with them. And He is in it with you.

God doesn't just call you to stand. He stands with you. He doesn't just test you. He strengthens you. He doesn't just watch the fire. He joins you in it. And when you come out, you won't just survive; you'll shine.

You'll come out with wisdom, depth, and revelation. You'll come out with greater clarity and a deeper understanding of who God is. The fire doesn't destroy your purpose—it forges it.

Reflection Questions

- What fiery trials have tested your faith recently?
- How has God preserved or strengthened you in the midst of difficulty?
- Are you standing firm or shrinking back

when pressure comes?

- What is God revealing about Himself and you in this season?
- How can I use my story of endurance to encourage someone else?

Let's Pray!

Dear Heavenly Father, thank You for being with me in the fire. When trials come, remind me of Psalm 27 that states, "You are a very present help in the time of trouble." I thank You that You are present, powerful, and preserving me. Give me strength to stand when it's hard, to believe when it hurts, and to trust You when I can't see the way forward. Use the fire to refine me, not define me. Let it shape my testimony and strengthen my purpose. I will not bow; I will not break. I will stand. In Jesus' name. Amen.

CHAPTER 9

Living Out Loud: The Cost of the Call

As the words on these pages resonate in your heart and your purpose begins to unfold, you may find yourself standing at a crossroads, counting the cost. And that's exactly where you're supposed to be.

Living out loud on purpose isn't just a bold declaration. It's a daily decision that comes with a cost. It will stretch you beyond what's comfortable and challenge you to surrender what's convenient. It may cost you your comfort, convenience, and sometimes even your connections. But don't mistake the struggle for failure; it's a sign that you're truly alive in your purpose.

Every sacrifice, every uncomfortable "yes," is part of the molding process. Purpose demands more from you because God intends to do more through you. The call of God is beautiful, but it is not without sacrifice. Yet, what you gain in Christ is far greater than anything you will ever give up.

When you live out loud on purpose, you're not just making noise; you're making a difference. And every step of obedience echoes in eternity.

Luke 9:23 lays it out clearly: "Whoever wants to be my disciple must deny themselves and take up their cross daily and follow me" (NIV).

This is not a casual invitation. It's a call to die to self in order to fully live in Him. Living out loud means dying daily to fear, ego, pride, and anything that stands in the way of obedience.

Following Christ isn't about ease; it's about endurance. While grace is free, the walk of faith is costly. It may cost you the approval of some, the applause of others, and the security of the familiar. But it will lead you straight into the center of God's will, and that is worth everything.

Romans 12:1 compels us: "Therefore, I urge you, brothers and sisters, in view of God's mercy, to offer your bodies as a living sacrifice, holy and pleasing to God—this is your true and proper worship."

True worship isn't just what you say or sing—it's what you surrender. Living out loud is an act of worship, and sacrifice is the sound that heaven hears.

Philippians 3:7-8 captures the mindset of a surrendered heart: "But whatever were gains to me I now consider loss for the sake of Christ. What is more, I consider everything a loss because of the surpassing worth of knowing Christ Jesus my Lord."

Paul understood the trade. When you live for Christ, what you let go of pales in comparison to what you gain. The call will cost you something, but never more than it's worth.

We live in a culture that promotes convenience over commitment and pleasure over purpose. But if you're going to live out loud on purpose, you'll have to go against the grain. You have to be willing to pay the price to carry the promise.

David said in 2 Samuel 24:24, "I will not offer to the Lord that which costs me nothing."

Obedience demands a cost—not just once, but daily.
- Daily surrender
- Daily trust
- Daily alignment

Purpose has a price, and many never reach it because they aren't willing to pay what it requires.

What Might the Call Cost You?
- Your comfort zone — God often calls you into the unknown, so you'll learn to rely fully on Him.
- Your schedule — Purpose rarely fits neatly into your planner.
- Your pride — Humility will be required, along with the release of needing to be understood by everyone.
- Your control — Faith means following, even when the path isn't clear.

- Your preferences — God's will often over-rides your personal desires.

Living Sacrificially Looks Like:

- Saying "yes" to God when everything in you wants to say "no"
- Trusting God's timing, even when it tests your patience
- Serving in hidden places when your heart longs to be seen
- Giving generously, even when it stretches your budget
- Choosing forgiveness when bitterness feels justified
- Staying faithful when walking away feels easier

The Beauty of Sacrifice

When you sacrifice for God, you're never losing—you're sowing. And what you sow in obedience, God multiplies in glory. Your sacrifice becomes someone else's blessing. Your obedience opens the door for others to encounter Jesus. Sacrifice isn't a sign of loss—it's evidence of love. It is a response to the One who gave everything for us.

Jesus Paid the Ultimate Cost

Let us never forget that we follow a Savior who paid the highest price. He gave His life so we could find ours. He carried the weight of the cross so we could carry the message of salvation. If He was willing to give everything for us, how can we hold anything back?

Living out loud on purpose means living sacrificially with joy. It means counting the cost and still saying yes. It means looking at the cross, then looking at your calling, and realizing—this is worth it. Because He is worth it.

Reflection Questions

- What is God asking you to sacrifice in this season?
- Where have you been hesitant to say "yes" to His call?
- How can you align your lifestyle with a posture of surrender?
- In what ways have you seen God honor your past obedience?
- What would it look like to fully trust God with the cost?

Let's Pray!

Gracious and Eternal God, thank You for the call You've placed on my life. Help me to live with open hands and a surrendered heart. Show me what I need to lay down so I can rise in Your purpose. Remind me that nothing I give up for You is ever wasted. Give me the strength to walk the narrow path, knowing that You walk it with me. I say yes to the cost because You are worth it all.

CHAPTER 10

Living Out Loud: Redefined

In today's culture, "living out loud" is often equated with bold self-expression—shouting one's truth, flaunting individuality, and demanding to be seen. But for the believer, living out loud means something entirely different. It's not about making noise for attention. It's about making a sound that carries eternal impact. The world says, "Look at me." The kingdom says, "Look at Him."

The cultural version of living out loud seeks to magnify self. The godly version seeks to magnify Christ. It's not about self-promotion—it's about divine purpose. And that purpose is rooted not in your platform, but in your obedience.

Romans 12:2 sets the foundation: "Do not conform to the pattern of this world but be transformed by the renewing of your mind. Then you will be able to test and approve what God's will is—His good, pleasing and perfect will" (NIV). Living out loud for God requires a transformed mind and a surrendered heart.

Matthew 5:14-16 reminds us: "You are the light of the world. A city set on a hill cannot be hidden... let your light shine before others, that they may see your good deeds and glorify your Father in heaven." Our visibility is meant to glorify God, not ourselves. We shine, not to spotlight our success, but to reflect His goodness.

There Is a Difference Between Cultural Noise and Kingdom Voice

Cultural noise demands attention, while the kingdom voice commands authority. Let's explore.

It is important to note that cultural noise performs and thrives on trends, being loud for the sake of being loud or constantly chasing clicks, likes, and validation. But at the end of the day, that attention doesn't always equal impact. The kingdom voice, on the other hand, commands authority. It doesn't have to be the loudest in the room, but when it speaks, the atmosphere shifts. Mountains move. Hearts are stirred. Chains are broken. This is the power of a voice that is backed by heaven.

Cultural noise promotes self, while the kingdom voice points to Jesus. Why is this so? Cultural noise tends to center its message around personal brand, influence, and image, ultimately elevating personality over purpose. It says, "Look at me," and thrives on recognition and applause.

In contrast, the kingdom voice is different. It points to Jesus. It doesn't seek a platform for self-glory but becomes a vessel for divine truth. It says, "Look to Him," and then redirects all praise back to the One who called, commissioned, and empowered it. While cultural noise is consumed with being seen, the kingdom voice is committed to making Jesus known.

Cultural noise stirs chaos, while the kingdom voice speaks peace. Cultural noise is loud, reactive, and emotionally charged—fueled by fear, offense, or confusion. It divides rather than unites, escalates conflict instead of resolving it, and thrives in atmospheres of unrest. It speaks first and thinks later, often leaving more harm than healing in its wake. But the kingdom voice speaks peace. It enters the storm with authority, not anxiety. It calms rather than provokes. It is anchored in truth and guided by wisdom. Where cultural noise agitates, the kingdom voice restores. It reminds the world that peace is not the absence of trouble but the presence of God.

Finally, cultural noise fades, but the kingdom voice remains. This point is critical to understand. In the fast-paced society we live in, cultural noise trends for a moment, sparks conversation, or goes viral. However, its influence is fleeting, momentary, and short-lived. In other words, it's here today, gone tomorrow, and quickly replaced by the next distraction or louder voice. The kingdom voice remains. It is sustainable and carries eternal weight because it is rooted in truth and aligned with heaven. It doesn't just make an impression—it leaves a legacy. Long after the noise dies down, the voice that speaks God's Word in season will still be bearing fruit, transforming lives, and echoing in eternity.

Cultural noise is often about being louder. The kingdom voice is about being clearer. One thrives on being heard; the other thrives on being heard from heaven.

John 17:16-18 echoes this truth: "They are not of the world, even as I am not of it. Sanctify them by the truth; your word is truth. As you sent me into the world, I have sent them into the world."

We are in the world but not of it. Our lives must reflect a higher standard, a holy difference.

What Living Out Loud for God Means

It means speaking the truth in love, even when that truth is uncomfortable or unpopular because truth, when rooted in love, brings freedom. It's reflecting grace under pressure, remaining steady and Christ-like in moments where others might break or retaliate. It's walking in integrity when no one else is watching, knowing that your character matters more than your image.

It is using your influence not to promote yourself, but to advance the kingdom—pointing others to Jesus through your words, witness, and walk.

Living out loud for God isn't about making noise. It's about making Him known.

It's Not About Being Seen; It's About Being Sent

The distinction is key: many seek visibility for validation. However, kingdom-minded believers understand that when God places them on display, it's not for applause—it's for assignment.

When God sends you, He equips you. And when He places you in the spotlight, it's to shine His truth, not your own.

Isaiah 60:1 declares: "Arise, shine, for your light has come, and the glory of the Lord rises upon you." You shine because His light has come upon you. You reflect the radiance of His glory, not the brilliance of self.

So, What Does That Look Like Practically?

Living out loud for God means being a bold witness for Christ without boasting—sharing your testimony with confidence, but never with arrogance. It's allowing your story to point others to God, not to self.

It means choosing to live authentically, holding fast to your values and convictions, even when compromise would be easier or more accepted. It means leading with a servant's heart—motivated not by position or recognition, but by love and humility that reflect the very character of Christ.

Practically, living out loud also means guarding your spirit, carrying joy and peace that defy external pressure, and refusing to let negativity or fear pull you out of alignment with God's promises. And it means speaking the truth, even when silence feels safer because truth is powerful, and your voice has purpose.

This is what it means to live out loud for God in real life: Consistent. Courageous. Anchored in purpose. You live out loud every time you forgive instead of retaliate, love instead of hate, and serve instead of seek status. You live out loud every time you choose faith over fear, and worship over worry.

When you live out loud God's way, your life becomes a walking sermon—preaching without a pulpit, ministering without a microphone. You become a living letter of grace, written not with ink but with the Spirit of the living God (2 Corinthians 3:3).

Reflection Questions

- Have you embraced the world's version of "living out loud" more than God's?
- In what ways can you reflect Christ more clearly through your words and actions?
- Are you seeking to be seen or to be sent?
- How can you ensure your influence points others to Jesus, not just to yourself?
- What mindset shift do you need to make to live out loud with purpose and purity?

Let's Pray!

Heavenly Father, help me to live out loud, not for attention, but for assignment. Let my life reflect Your glory, not my own. Transform my mind so I can clearly discern the difference between the world's noise and Your voice.

CHAPTER 11

The Fruit That Remains: Legacy of Loud Living

Living out loud isn't just about today's impact—it's about tomorrow's inheritance. It's not about the noise we make in the moment, but the fruit we leave in the lives of others. Living out loud on purpose means planting seeds of faith, love, and truth that will produce a harvest long after our voices fade. A loud life is not defined by echoes in the crowd, but by eternal evidence in the kingdom. John 15:16 says, "You did not choose me, but I chose you and appointed you so that you might go and bear fruit—fruit that will last—and so that whatever you ask in my name the Father will give you" (NIV).

This is not a temporary calling. It's a divine appointment to live a life that multiplies. Jesus didn't save us for momentary significance. He called us to eternal impact. Your legacy is not what you accumulate. It's what you activate in others. It's not about the titles you've held, but the testimonies you've left behind. Your loud living becomes a witness, a trail, a roadmap for others to follow.

It's your children watching your consistency. It's your community experiencing your compassion. It's heaven recording your faithfulness. It's not about what people say at your funeral. It's what lives on because of your life.

Galatians 5:22-23 outlines what this fruit looks like: "But the fruit of the Spirit is love, joy, peace, forbearance, kindness, goodness, faithfulness, gentleness and self-control. Against such things, there is no law."

These qualities are not personality traits; they are evidence of a Spirit-filled life. Loud living isn't always about speaking, but it is always about bearing. Your fruit speaks volumes long after your words fade.

Psalm 92:12-14 reminds us: "The righteous will flourish like a palm tree, they will grow like a cedar of Lebanon; planted in the house of the Lord, they will flourish in the courts of our God. They will still bear fruit in old age, they will stay fresh and green."

Living out loud doesn't expire with age; it matures with time. The older you grow, the richer your fruit. When you're rooted in God, you're never too young to bear fruit, and never too old to remain fruitful. Legacy is built in layers. It's not formed in a single moment, but in a series of intentional choices.

Every word of encouragement, every seed sown in generosity, every act of faith, every quiet moment of obedience—all of it matters. Every stand for truth, every whispered prayer in the secret place becomes a building block in the legacy you leave behind. These layers may seem small in the moment, but over time, they create something lasting. Something eternal. Loud living leaves fruit that testifies.

People may forget your name, but they'll remember how you made them feel. They'll remember the peace you carried, the truth you spoke, the way you served, and the Jesus you revealed. A life lived out loud on purpose makes heaven louder—and hell more nervous.

How Do We Bear Fruit That Remains?

Fruit that remains isn't produced by accident—it's the result of a life deeply rooted in Christ and intentionally focused on what truly matters.

1. Stay Connected to the Vine

John 15:5 says, "I am the vine; you are the branches. If you remain in me and I in you, you will bear much fruit; apart from me you can do nothing."

There is no spiritual growth, lasting impact, or true transformation without intimacy with Him. Our connection to Christ is the source of everything fruitful in our lives. It's not about striving; it's about abiding.

2. Live with Eternity in Mind

Every day presents the opportunity to either sow to the flesh or the Spirit. Fruit that lasts is born from choices made with heaven in view. Temporary actions have eternal consequences. What we do now echoes forever. Living out loud on purpose means making daily decisions that align with the bigger picture—God's kingdom agenda.

3. Invest in People, Not Just Platforms

In a culture obsessed with numbers, visibility, and influence, we're reminded that the true measure of impact isn't how many follow us—it's how many grow because of us. Fruit that remains shows up in changed lives, healed hearts, and people empowered to walk in their God-given purpose. You don't need a stage to make a difference—you need a surrendered heart and a willingness to pour into others.

4. Choose Consistency Over Charisma

We live in a world impressed by talent and charm, but fruit that remains comes through faithfulness. Charisma may draw a crowd, but consistency builds character. It's not how loud you are in the moment that matters; it's how faithfully you show up when no one's clapping, and how steadfastly you walk with God when no one's watching.

5. Let Your Life Preach Louder Than Your Lips

You don't need a microphone to make a mark. A life that reflects Christ speaks volumes. It's in how you love, forgive, serve, and stand. A fruitful life is one where your walk backs up your words and your presence carries the fragrance of Jesus wherever you go.

Fun fact: I absolutely love a good fragrance—one that is light, refreshing, and leaves a lasting impression. I'm frequently asked, "What is that fragrance you're wearing?" There's something powerful about a scent that lingers even after you've left the room. And in many ways, that's what it's like when you bear fruit that remains. When your life is rooted in Christ and lived out loud on purpose, you carry a spiritual fragrance—one that leaves a lasting impact long after the moment has passed.

People may not always remember your name, your title, or your words. But they'll remember how you made them feel, how you pointed them to Jesus, and how your life reflected something deeper.

Fruit that remains is the aroma of a life lived well for God's glory. Let's be clear: you don't need a big stage to bear big fruit. Some of the most powerful legacies were built in kitchens, classrooms, neighborhoods, and other hidden places. Sometimes, the most lasting legacy comes from the quiet consistency of daily surrender. It comes from loving well, giving generously, praying fervently, and serving faithfully, even when no one is watching. Because fruit that remains doesn't come from striving. It comes from abiding. It's the result of walking closely with God, day after day, season after season.

Reflection Questions

- What kind of fruit is your life producing?
- How are you investing in others beyond yourself?
- In what ways are you building a legacy that points to Christ?
- What seeds do you need to start sowing today for tomorrow's harvest?
- Who in your life is already being nourished by the fruit you have cultivated?

Let's Pray!

Heavenly Father, thank You for choosing and appointing me to bear fruit that remains. Help me to live with eternity in mind. Teach me to sow seeds of righteousness, faith, and love that will bless generations. May my legacy be one of faithfulness, impact, and obedience. Let my life echo Your glory and multiply Your goodness. May every fruit of my life bring You honor. In Jesus' name. Amen.

CHAPTER 12

David Was a Morning Person

Throughout the psalms, David gives us intimate insight into how he started his day—with intention, worship, and open expectation. He made the morning a sacred space to seek the Lord, speak with Him, and listen. David's mornings weren't rushed or random. They were focused and full of faith.

Psalm 5:3 says, "In the morning, O Lord, You will hear my voice; In the morning I will prepare [a prayer and a sacrifice] for You and watch and wait [for You to speak to my heart]" (AMP). David didn't just pray—he prepared. He postured his heart before God with intentionality and expectation. Living out loud begins in the secret place, long before it shows up in public.

David understood something we often forget: mornings matter. The way we start our day determines the pace and posture of everything that follows. Mornings are where we align with heaven, receive daily instruction, and offer our first fruit of time and attention to the One who sustains us. For David, the morning wasn't just a time of day; it was a time of dedication.

Psalm 63:1 echoes this rhythm: "O God, You are my God; early will I seek You; My soul thirsts for You; My flesh longs for You in a dry and thirsty land where there is no water." David's language was never casual; it was desperate. His mornings were fueled by hunger and thirst for God's presence.

This kind of early seeking speaks to dependency. David recognized his limitations. He knew that before he made any decisions, faced any battles, or engaged with any people, he had to first engage with God. Morning devotion was his weapon and his wisdom. He entered each day anchored, because he started it surrendered.

In a world filled with distractions and demands,

choosing to begin your day with God is a declaration: "I trust You with this day. I need You more than I need control." It is the intentional act of giving God the first moments, the first thoughts, the first whispers of worship—before texts, emails, or social media have a chance to set the tone.

David wasn't alone in this practice. Scripture is full of people who encountered God early:

- Abraham rose early to obey God's instruction (Genesis 22:3).
- Moses met with God early on Mount Sinai (Exodus 34:4).
- Jesus Himself withdrew early to pray (Mark 1:35).

There's something sacred about the stillness of morning, the quiet before the noise, the clarity before the clutter. In that sacred space, God speaks. He reveals. He restores.

Living Out Loud Starts in the Morning

- It starts with *surrender*—laying down our agendas to hear God's.

- It starts with *connection*—seeking His face before we face the world.
- It starts with *direction*—listening for His instruction before we act.

David's mornings weren't perfect, but they were *pursuing*. He set the tone of his day by putting God first, and that practice made his life fruitful, focused, and full of grace—even in chaos. It didn't keep him from hardship, but it kept his heart aligned with God through it.

David teaches us that consistency with God in the quiet place creates confidence in the public place. His morning voice became a lifelong echo—shaping songs, victories, and even repentance. The same David who said, "In the morning You will hear my voice," is the one God called "a man after My own heart."

Benefits of Morning Devotion

One of the greatest benefits of morning devotion is that it sets the tone for a life lived out loud for God and on purpose. In those quiet, early moments with Him, your heart aligns with heaven, and your spirit is strengthened to face the day with clarity and conviction. Morning devotion equips you to be a bold witness for Christ without boasting—anchoring your confidence in God, not in self, and reminding you that your story is meant to point others to Him. It cultivates authenticity, helping you hold fast to your values and convictions, even when compromise seems easier.

Spending time in God's presence reshapes your posture, empowering you to lead with a servant's heart, motivated by love, not status; grounded in humility, not performance.

Morning devotion guards your spirit, allowing joy and peace to rise above the pull of negativity, anxiety, and fear. It fills you with the courage to speak truth, even when silence feels more comfortable. In devotion, you're reminded that your voice carries purpose and your words carry weight.

Ultimately, morning devotion doesn't just prepare you for the day—it prepares you to live the day well: Consistent. Courageous. Anchored in purpose.

You don't have to be a "morning person" by personality, but you can be one in principle. It's not about being an early riser. It's about being an intentional seeker. Whether your morning starts at 4 a.m. or 9 a.m., what matters is what you prioritize when your day begins. It's about who you seek first.

When we neglect our mornings with God, we often find ourselves chasing clarity, scrambling for peace, and reacting to chaos, rather than walking in confidence. However, when we begin our day with the Lord, we step into alignment. We move from reaction to revelation. From confusion to clarity. From drifting to direction.

Starting your day with God is how you begin to live out loud with wisdom, power, and peace. It's how you position your life to move in sync with heaven. It's how you ensure that your loud living has holy direction.

Reflection Questions
- How do you currently start your day?
- In what ways might you be rushing past God's invitation to meet with Him?

- What distractions do you need to remove to make room for morning devotion?
- How might a focused morning with God shift the rest of your day?
- What can you commit to doing differently tomorrow morning?

Let's Pray!

Eternal God, my heavenly Father, thank You for meeting me in the morning. Teach me to prioritize Your presence above all else. As I prepare for each day, help me come before You with expectation and humility. Open my heart to hear Your voice, receive Your peace, and walk in Your wisdom. May every morning become an altar of connection and commissioning. In Jesus' name. Amen.

CHAPTER 13

The Most Powerful Church Is an Intentional Church

We've talked about purpose, power, identity, and endurance, but what happens when individuals committed to living out loud on purpose come together in unity? They become the most powerful force on Earth. They become the church. Not just a building, but a body. Not just a service, but a strategy. The most powerful church is not the biggest or the flashiest—it's the most *intentional*.

Matthew 16:18 reminds us of Jesus' words: "I will build My church, and the gates of hell shall not prevail against it." That promise is attached to a church that knows who it is and what it's called to do. It's not a passive church. It's not a reactive church. It is intentionally rooted in truth, led by the Spirit, and mobilized by purpose.

Intentional churches don't wait for revival; they cultivate it. Intentional churches don't chase trends; they create culture through the Word of God. Intentional churches don't fill seats; they fill lives with the presence and power of Jesus.

A powerful church begins with powerful people who live on purpose every day, who show up, speak up, and love deeply. When a congregation is made up of individuals who are living out loud in their own callings, the church becomes an unstoppable force.

What does an intentional church look like?

An intentional church is one that goes beyond surface-level gatherings and truly lives out its mission. It disciples, not just entertains. It is committed to spiritual growth over emotional hype.

It empowers, not just instructs—equipping believers

to walk in their God-given authority, not merely filling them with information.

It mobilizes, not just gathers—sending people out to be the hands and feet of Jesus in their communities and beyond.

It loves without limits—embracing the broken, the lost, and the overlooked with the unconditional love of Christ.

It leads with integrity—modeling Christlike character behind the scenes, as well as on the platform. And above all, it prays with fervor—relying not on human strength, but on the power of God to lead, sustain, and transform.

Acts 2:42-47 gives us a glimpse of the early church. They were devoted to teaching, fellowship, breaking of bread, and prayer. Their intentional unity resulted in miraculous power, radical generosity, and explosive growth. That wasn't a coincidence; it was commitment. They lived out loud together.

Ephesians 4:16 says, "From Him the whole body,

joined and held together by every supporting liga-
ment, grows and builds itself up in love, as each part
does its work." Every part matters. Your purpose
isn't only personal; it's *corporate*. Your loud living
contributes to the symphony of kingdom impact.

The church doesn't need more performers. It needs
more participants. It doesn't need more celebrities. It
needs more servants. It doesn't need to be louder in
volume. It needs to be clearer in purpose.

The most powerful church is intentional in its pursuit
of God, its discipleship of people, and its advance-
ment of the kingdom. And that church starts with
you.

Reflection Questions

- How are you contributing to the intentionality of your church?
- In what ways can you live more purposefully
  within your faith community?
- What part of the body has God called you to
  strengthen?
- How can you help your church be more effective in making disciples?

- Are you showing up with intention or merely out of routine?

Let's Pray!

Heavenly Father, thank You for calling me into Your body—the church. Help me to live and serve with intention. Strengthen me to play my part, to love my community, and to advance Your kingdom. Make us a church that's not only powerful in word, but intentional in deed. Let our lives reflect Your glory together. In Jesus' name. Amen.

You Did That on Purpose!

Now, we return to where we began: God has always held a divine plan for your life, written before time began—and He invites you to live it out with holy intention and unwavering purpose.

From Genesis to Revelation, the entire Bible reveals a story rich with masterful design and divine intention. Every line, plot, twist, promise, and prophecy points to a God who moves with purpose and calls us to do the same. You were never an accident. You were never overlooked. You have always been a part of His intentions. You have always been a part of His plan.

"Thine eyes did see my substance, yet being unperfect; and in thy book all my members were written, which in continuance were fashioned, when as yet there was none of them" (Psalm 139:16).

Even before you took your first breath, God had already mapped out your days. His blueprint included your gifts, calling, and voice. He created you on purpose, for purpose.

Living out loud on purpose is not a one-time decision; it's a way of life. It means waking up each day determined to rise, speak, serve, and show up with clarity and conviction. You were not created to live small, silent, or scared. You were born to carry light, to speak truth, and to walk boldly in the purpose God uniquely assigned to you.

For me, this book has been a journey—a call to shake off my own complacency and insecurities and step into my divine assignment. So, whether your stage is a sanctuary or a break room, whether you're leading in worship or whispering prayers in the midnight hour, you've been commissioned to live boldly and purposefully. Purpose is not reserved for the famous or the flawless. It's found in the hands of the faithful.

Why? Because purpose is revealed in the ordinary. And when ordinary people choose to walk with extraordinary faith, heaven touches the earth, and nothing stays the same.

"For I know the thoughts that I think toward you, saith the LORD, thoughts of peace, and not of evil, to give you an expected end" (Jeremiah 29:11).

So, what now?

You *live*. Not later. Not someday. *Now.*

Live on purpose.

Live with courage.

Live with conviction.

Live with clarity.

Live out loud.

The world needs your light. The church needs your voice. And heaven is cheering you on. Let your life declare what your heart has always known: "I was born for this."

A Prayer for Commissioning

Father, I thank You for every person who has walked through these pages. I declare that this is not the end but the beginning of a bold, powerful, and purposeful life. Let Your Spirit lead them; let Your Word ground them, and let Your love propel them.

Awaken dreams. Break off fear. Release clarity. Fill them with holy fire. May their lives echo the sound of heaven and shake the gates of hell. They were born for this, and they will live out loud for Your glory. In Jesus' name. Amen.

The Visual Metaphor
of Living Out Loud on Purpose

The cover of *Living Out Loud on Purpose* is a visual metaphor of the spiritual transformation that occurs when you stop shrinking, start shining, and boldly walk in alignment with God's divine plan.

The front cover, with its vivid paint splashes, represents a life filled with motion, emotion, and potential—but lacking clarity. It captures what it feels like to exist without truly living: colorful, expressive, yet undefined. It mirrors the season many go through—playing supportive roles, staying silent in rooms where they were meant to speak, hiding behind expectations instead of walking in purpose. This is what life looks like before we find our voice, embrace our God-given identity, and begin walking in alignment with heaven.

The back cover tells a different story—the one God always intended. The same colors now take on new form and meaning, transforming into a **flower, butterfly, tree, and bird,** each a symbol of a believer awakened to their divine calling:

- The **flower** represents spiritual blooming— what happens when you stop hiding and begin to flourish in the soil of God's Word (Psalm 1:3).
- The **butterfly** reflects the beauty of transformation through Christ, as we are renewed in mind and spirit (Romans 12:2).
- The **tree** symbolizes strength, stability, and a life rooted in purpose, bearing fruit that impacts generations (Jeremiah 17:7–8).
- The **bird** embodies freedom in Christ and the boldness to rise above fear and walk by faith (Isaiah 40:31).

Together, these images reflect what happens when you choose to live out loud on purpose—with clarity, courage, and conviction. You stop echoing the world and start embodying the kingdom.

This cover is more than a design—it's a declaration. It says:

"I will not shrink to fit spaces God called me to transform. I will rise. I will speak. I will live on purpose."

And just like the message inside the book, it invites every reader to move from invisibility to intentionality, from hiding to holy boldness, from silence to significance—through the power of knowing who you are, whose you are, and why you're here.

About the Author

Karen F. Hatcher, M.S. in Marriage and Family Therapy, is a National Evangelist in the Church Of God In Christ. A devoted wife, mother, and grandmother, she blends her passion for faith, family, and service with wisdom and authenticity.

Evangelist Hatcher has dedicated her life to strengthening individuals and families by integrating mental health, spirituality, and biblical principles. Her mission is to empower the body of Christ to fulfill God's purpose in this generation, boldly proclaiming that the kingdom of heaven is at hand and urging believers to prepare for the soon-coming King. She serves as the First Lady of Miracle Temple of Deliverance Church Of God In Christ in Louisville, Kentucky, alongside her husband, Bishop Gabriel J. Hatcher Sr. Together, they are blessed with three children—Gabriel II, Sarah, and Rachel—and eleven grandchildren.

Credits and References

- Stephen R. Covey, *The 7 Habits of Highly Effective People*, Free Press, 1989. Quote: "Responsibility is the ability to respond."
- Biblegateway.com was consulted for cross-referencing scripture in multiple translations.
- Some thematic inspiration drawn from teachings, sermons, and writings of contemporary Christian leaders and theologians. Any paraphrased concepts are acknowledged with gratitude and reverence for their contribution to the body of Christ.

Sources Cited

Scripture References (King James Version, unless otherwise noted)

- Psalm 139 – God's intimate knowledge, presence, and intentionality.
- Jeremiah 29:11 – God's plan and hope for the future.

- Acts 1:8, John 14:26, John 16:13, Galatians 5:22–23 – The Holy Spirit and the fruit of the Spirit.

- Proverbs 3:5-6, Proverbs 15:1, Proverbs 15:22, Proverbs 19:11 – Wisdom and guidance.

- Matthew 5:14–16, Matthew 3:17, Matthew 5:16 – Light of the world, divine affirmation.

- Romans 12:1–2, Romans 8:29, Romans 12:2 – Transformation and renewal.

- John 10:10, John 17:16–18 – Abundant life and sanctification.

- 1 Peter 2:9, 1 Corinthians 11:1 – Identity in Christ and godly leadership.

- James 1:2–4, James 1:19 – Wisdom in trials and control of the tongue.

- Isaiah 60:1, Isaiah 64:8 – God's light and the potter's hand.

- Joshua 24:15 – Commitment to serve the Lord.

- Galatians 6:9, Galatians 2:20 – Perseverance and crucified life.

- 2 Timothy 1:7 – Spirit of power, love, and a sound mind.
- Revelation 12:11 – Victory through testimony.
- Psalm 46:1, Psalm 92:12–14 – God as a refuge and flourishing in righteousness.
- 2 Samuel 24:24 – Cost of true worship.
- Daniel 3 – The faith of Shadrach, Meshach, and Abednego.
- Genesis 1:31, Genesis 37–50 – Creation's goodness and Joseph's journey.
- Ecclesiastes 3:1 – Seasons and timing.
- 1 Samuel 16 – David's anointing.
- John 3:30 – Humility and God's increase.
- Luke 12:48 – Responsibility with greater blessings.
- 1 Peter 4:10 – Stewardship of gifts.
- 2 Corinthians 4:8–9, 2 Corinthians 4:17 – Resilience in trials.
- Ephesians 2:10 – Created for good works.

Quotations from Other Authors

Stephen R. Covey – "Responsibility is the ability to respond."

Additional References

Greek Word Study: *"Perissos"* (περισσὸν) – John 10:10, meaning abundant, exceeding, or beyond measure.